In a Ribbon of Rhythm

LEBOGANG MASHILE

In a Ribbon of Rhythm

MU LOATSE
arts heritage trust

Oshun

Mutloatse Arts Heritage Trust

1 Steyn Street

Observatory

Johannesburg 2198

Email: mutloatse@mweb.co.za

Oshun

Published by Oshun Books

An imprint of Struik Publishers

(a division of New Holland Publishing (South Africa) (Pty) Ltd)

Cornelis Struik House

80 McKenzie Street

Cape Town 8001

New Holland Publishing is a member of Johnnic Communications Ltd.

First published in 2005

10 9 8 7 6 5 4 3 2

Publishing manager: Michelle Matthews

Co-publisher: Mothobi Mutloatse

Editor: Don Mattera

Cover and book design: Greenteabag Design at www.greenteabag.co.za

Production manager: Valerie Kömmer

Reproduction by Hirt & Carter Cape (Pty) Ltd

Printed and bound by Paarl Print, Oosterland Street, Paarl, South Africa

ISBN 978 177007 0455

www.oshunbooks.co.za

To Mama, Mpho and Tshepo

Contents

This morning

This morning rolls in with rain shadows
And a cool voice crisply shaking the last
Of winter's whirlwinds to a standstill
There will be no pain this morning
It has been sucked into the sky
From the other side of forever
Where the ghosts of our former selves
Will bind their dreams from its sinew
Their tears keep our dreams from falling apart

This morning the Gods have shown us their teeth
We grin and violently shiver into one another
Eyes closed
Mouths open
Hands tied to tomorrows and yesterdays
And promises we may never keep

This morning I present myself
To the light that bounces from iced people
To the chills that shape a human body into a human being
To every person spinning in a moment forgotten
Except for the most searing touches of love
We are bare teeth glistening
Winter mornings hoping
That somewhere past forever
The world is listening

My imagined community

In our separate corners
Bound together by
Slavery
Colonisation
Poverty
AIDS
Drugs
Abuse
And ideas that are not backed
By Anglo-Arab conglomerates or American aid
We are holding pieces of the blueprint
For the world that the most blessed will inhabit

We are not fighting
Those who have lived on oceans of tears and suffering
We are fighting the silence
They have left on our palates
That chokes our anger
Suffocates indignation
Slaps the taste of the truth out of the mouth
Until the bitterness of spinelessness
Grows sweet
As the 4 x 4 dreams of black babies
In Harlem
Soweto
Port Limon
Dakar
Sweeter even than freedom

Style

It is the very liquid soul that oozes from these pores
To light the sidewalks with our magic beyond the distant shores
It is the joy from which the laughter of the dying is drawn
Style is in the essence of my people

We walk tall in every creed and shape and language known to man
We walk tall and touch the Gods with every step upon this land
We walk tall into our futures burning our memories into the sand
Because style is in the bodies of my people

And when we move to any groove we shake the earth around the sun
Ask for the tricks that dip our hips we'll tell you rhythm makes blood run
Back to the source African booties know the answers and when I'm done
I'll tell you style is in the movements of my people

And though we breathe in acid jazz our voices rise in melody
To sing through blues where sorrows ride the waves of tranquillity
In a house of music funky is the place we're going to be
So be the bass in my mbaqanga be my tongue as a I ululate
Move the feet that move the world to kwaito beats at any rate
And trip not when hip-hop lifts you above mundane things
Because the birds have been singing that we're too fly not to have wings

But they'll tell you that we have no hope
Lazy bastards dying from HIV
That this bloody continent's a joke
Destroyed by wars and apathy
That money rules the world

My people merely a casualty
To forces much more slick
And shadows with more power
To titans in the face of which we can only cower

But we know the force that rules the world
Derives its power from our dance
When my people express their beauty
The whole world goes into a trance
When we create we shape the planet
It's only through voice that we have a chance
Because style is in the music of my people

So wear your colours with pride
Sing your spirits unplugged
We'll use the hands that built our art
To build ourselves with love
Always remember that you carry your style in your blood
Because style is in the survival of my people

The most powerful (black) woman in the world

The most powerful (black) woman in the world
Stares out from eyes that see the planet
And salivates for the feel of human bones
Cracking between her teeth

She will be remembered as the one
Who gave us permission to climb
To the highest echelons of evil
And show that we are not the same

Tomorrow's daughters

I want to write a poem
About pretty black girls
Who don't relax and lie their dreams away
Voices that curl
The straight edges of history
Hair thin slices of a movement
Turning the world kinky
I respect the disciplined silent screamers
Who expose the holes
Emily Dickinson, I am climbing through
To your wooden shed of isolation
Where the robin's song
Robbed you of your sanity
I revere people to my own detriment
Perhaps you did too
But when I enter your hallowed hearth
Please don't turn me away
I want to show pretty black girls
How to look at their hearts
With eyes blaring at full blast
The way you did
Together we can build a bridge
To the promise in their faces
And pull them towards poems
By pretty black girls
Wearing crowns of change

Inside outsider

Home is a foreign land
That hurls the might of its confusion around the world
Strangers believe they know my bruises
The smallness of boxes they call eyes
And woo them into a false comfort

I will not live in boxes
They are not my home
Home is laughter
Home is rounded figures
Home is a sharpened mental weapon
To be wielded against foreigners of the spirit

I am tired of being different
My feet burn from the fires of those
Who have been anointed
With the certainty of origins

I will wander the earth
In search of my tribe
Or build it from the shreds of boxes
With my own hands

Kedi's song

While shooting the first series of L'Atitude *for SABC1, I had the opportunity to visit the town of Excelsior in the Free State. Thirty years ago, an international sex scandal rocked this small, deeply racist community. Prominent white men were discovered to be sleeping with their black domestic workers, and both groups were arrested for violation of the Immorality Act. News of the case spread worldwide. President Hendrik Verwoerd eventually threw the case out of court to avoid further embarrassment for the apartheid regime.*

The people of Excelsior are friendly and welcoming, but to this day, people refuse to speak about the case. The whispers, however, are still alive and well. Young people in the black community with light complexions are often labeled as products of illicit unions between black and white. In this way, the silence of the scandal is given a powerful, living voice through the hues of defenseless community members.

When profanity clamoured unto seduction's breast
When power devoured and nightfall offered no rest
These women sweep the whispers beneath their children's skins
Suckled on hushed voices
Shaded by history's sins
Even as her voice is captive,
Her skin will always sing:

"I am the colour of fresh bread
The colour of winter leaves
The colour of memories burned
They colour my misdeeds

The colour of earth stolen
The colour of pride broken
The colour of secrets spoken
The colour of pale tokens

But when I sing
It's with the sun on my tongue and Sesotho beating in my chest
When I sing
It's for the love of a life I can't touch without fingers of regret
I sing
For what I can't remember but my body won't let me forget
I sing for the embers of legacy
I sing because I have nothing left"

Love is elastic

When I am closed
Used up
You are stretched at your fullest width
Ready to give
I want to jump
Into you
And feel this life
As you do
Perhaps then
I could give as you do
Perhaps then
I could live as you do

Every child, my child

Every child, my child is wrapped in a ribbon of rhythm
Every child, my child is wrapped in a ribbon of rhythm
Every child, my child is wrapped in a ribbon of rhythm,
Wrapped in a ribbon of rhythm,
Wrapped in a ribbon of rhythm

Every child, my child is wrapped in a ribbon of rhythm
Every child, my child is wrapped in a ribbon of rhythm
Every child, my child is wrapped in a ribbon of rhythm,
Wrapped in a ribbon of rhythm,
Wrapped in a ribbon of rhythm

Our future hangs on the present's legacies
Life is a puzzle held together by the air we breathe
If hope were breath, with every second of time
We could conceive
Of a life where love is not betrayed by mirages
Of concrete hierarchies
And other fallacies

I've been told that these promises come wrapped in satin skin
And the force that brings them forth
Is inherent in these vessels we use
To peruse this web-like journey of existence

Some are guided by words woven with rhythm
Blessed are those guided by words woven with a ribbon of rhythm
The blessed are guided by words moulded by the light of their vision

Woven with a ribbon of rhythm
Their souls dance through transitions

Life is a gift from our ancestors that we borrow from our children
Blessed are those guided by words moulded by the light of their vision
Life is a gift from our ancestors that we borrow from our children
Blessed are those guided by words woven with a ribbon of rhythm

Every child should know the hands that receive them
In that instant believe them
To be the perfection that will fulfil their greatest destiny
My child will know deception and rage can be converted to pages
Where reality can heal in the realm of fantasy

Every child should know that they are a gift
A present fulfilment of wishes
To know the love of growth manifest in the love of another
My child will know they once were a dream,
My mind's eye could only conceive
Once my spirit was strengthened into something bolder

Every child should know the scope of their greatness
Is contained in the weightless
Inconvertible light that is their truest being
My child will know that boxes like race, class and gender
Are fated to be transcended in the face of a limitless self that is free

Every child, my child is wrapped in a ribbon of rhythm
Every child, my child is wrapped in a ribbon of rhythm
Every child, my child is wrapped in a ribbon of rhythm,
Wrapped in a ribbon of rhythm,
Wrapped in a ribbon of rhythm

Every child, my child is wrapped in a ribbon of rhythm
Every child, my child is wrapped in a ribbon of rhythm
Every child, my child is wrapped in a ribbon of rhythm,
Wrapped in a ribbon of rhythm,
Wrapped in a ribbon of rhythm

Every child is the strand that binds the tethered edges of community
Whether we shape shift, makeshift illusions
reality strives for something better
In the form of our children
We've got to build them a base that starts with the skies
So they can reach for the sons and daughters
Who'll be brought through the currents of fantasies
That we only touch the edges of

Every child, my child beings of light and wisdom
Sees that the colours of beauty flow through a jagged prism
That character grows through fear suffering and intuition
So never strive for comfort because life begins on its fringes
Never blame another for the corners you might find yourself in
You'll tie a noose around your pride forever being a victim
Never weigh another against the values you choose

Some demons plague you till death
Others walk with you to free you
Some demons plague you till death
Others walk with you to free you
Some demons plague you till death
Others walk with you to free you

And if you give them a chance with time
You might break through to be you

And be true to the song that was written on your palm
To the path that was crafted in your heart before long
This moment will be nothing but a memory
Shining forth from a blackened history
Like the stars an after-burning eulogy
To this instant that once glued you to me

And I live to honour the child in me
And she lives to honour the child in we
And we live to honour the child in thee

Every child, my child is wrapped in a ribbon of rhythm
Every child, my child is wrapped in a ribbon of rhythm
Every child, my child is wrapped in a ribbon of rhythm,
Wrapped in a ribbon of rhythm,
Wrapped in a ribbon of rhythm

Every child, my child is wrapped in a ribbon of rhythm
Every child, my child is wrapped in a ribbon of rhythm
Every child, my child is wrapped in a ribbon of rhythm,
Wrapped in a ribbon of rhythm,
Wrapped in a ribbon of rhythm

Desert child

The sand swallows my tears
So I carry them inside
Behind fragile baby flesh
And jaded adult eyes
In my tribe we raise each other
I have never been a child
The drunken lullabies of the streets keep me wild
Feral and intelligent
Naughty yet benevolent
I sleep to feel my innocence
Too young to see in retrospect
The dust turns up rose quartz
As my neighbours down beer quarts
To wet the deserts in their hearts
And bind their broken brittle parts
At night, I dream of running beyond the sand dunes
Drawing my face in the stars
Riding bareback on the moon
I don't speak my dreams
Fearing the softness of things unseen
By day they cushion me
From the ageing wars of my reality
My thoughts are sharp like light reflecting on sharded glass
Cutting the hands that feed me
Hoping their blood will lead me
To the desert's end

A tangled web of rainbows

I adore the night. It reveals the many different shades of blackness. Shy midnight blues exude thoughtfulness and nobility. Sensual purples invite gentle probing from fingertips much like bruises. Pitch black, as solid as the heart, grows into a mass of increasing impenetrability, like my father's retreats into liquor, jazz and memories.

Ostracism has its shades as well. That which is exotic is seen as an inviting challenge to the adventurer, but another kind calls up that which is all too familiar.

People who make their homes in foreign lands are not trying to recreate the ones they have left behind, but unless an individual comes to terms with every home they have ever known, the painfully familiar has a way of hooking on to a person and dutifully following them wherever their path may lead.

When I come to corners where it is difficult to find respect for myself, I remember who I was when I was eleven. I was proud, strong, intelligent, assertive and funny. A natural leader, I had my own definitive ideas on feminism. These came to life in a picture I drew in crayon of a woman in a business suit juggling a pot, a baby, a briefcase and the planet. She was inspired by my mother. I won contests for my writing long before I would claim it as my life's passion. I had black friends, white friends and I spoke freely about race, politics and my firm belief that the school's gym teacher was sexist.

I was magic.

I was schizophrenic. I felt unwanted and unloved at home, and I battled with my parents, especially my mother, as a daily ritual.

I often thought that my sisters were agents sent from forces in the universe that despised me with the mission to torture me into complete submission.

My prayers to God were full of fear.

I was American in my world, listened to Queen Latifah, wore Nikes and loved roller-skating more than anything else in the world.

I was an exiled South African in my house.

Home, for my parents, was a place far away from where we were living as a family.

The thought of leaving my home, America, Providence, Rhode Island for this place was a heart-shattering nightmare.

The day that Nelson Mandela was released from prison, a life lesson was carved into my heart.

I did not celebrate with the rest of the world.

I cried and called all of my friends who were supposed to come to my birthday party and cancelled.

My father, in his excitement about the prospect of returning to the only land he had ever known as home, had suggested that I go to boarding school with all of the finesse of a man who had spent the greater part of his childhood in boarding schools when he was not being beaten by his father.

For him, the closeness of intimacy left no room for tact.

It was brutal. I imagine that during the course of his tumultuous abusive childhood, boarding school became a place of safety.

In my world, I could not imagine being further away from home than I already was inside my own skin.

School was the heaven that saved me. There were no straight lines in Mrs Sasken's class.

The desks were arranged in a horseshoe pattern that hugged an inner circle of desks.

Later in the year, we patterned ourselves into clusters of four or five, like satellites bound together in a constellation spanning the entire room.

We were a community of equals. Even now, I cannot remember a single lesson, a game plan of grammar and spelling for the day, but I do remember savouring the unexpectedness of learning, spontaneity, and creativity.

While the other classes rehashed the same old green and red decorations with tired snowmen made out of cotton balls at Christmas, we ate potato latkes with apple butter.

When the school board introduced plans for school uniform, we put posters on the walls of the corridors in defiance.

Later on, we were forced to take them down. Our principal, a closet fascist, banned our protest for being a fire hazard.

I began keeping a journal in Mrs Sasken's class. It was my first space of free thought, the first time I had a collection of my ideas and feelings down on paper.

It didn't feel like school, it felt like an adventure and of course we brimmed with confidence and brilliance.

We were fifth graders. We owned E.W. Flynn Model Elementary School, having evolved from primitive babyish first graders to the regality of pre-pubescent seniority.

The year 1990 fleshed itself out into one of the best years of my life without my even knowing it.

In South Africa, my generation is bearing the first fruits of freedom.

We are the legacy of hope and battles, some won, some still being fought. Included in this post-Apartheid kaleidoscope is a small group of in betweeners. Young people who bear the tastes and colours of the many different countries around the world in which they were born, the offspring of parents who did not know when or if they would ever return to the beloved country of their birth.

South Africa now extends the possibility of world travel to all of its citizens, provided that one has the access via a big purse or even bigger dreams.

Children born in other parts of the world are similar, but very different to us. It is a new history.

We bear the scars of exile: of forced silences and dislocation.

Our childhoods were spent, in part, marinating in the frustrations of isolation, immigration and the struggle against Apartheid. We are foreigners in the countries of our births and in the lands that we now call home, including South Africa.

We are an anomaly that is an intrinsic thread in the fabric of South Africa's history, one of many contradictions in a complicated national identity still in its infancy.

10 February 1990 slid firmly into the shortest coldest month of the calendar year in the United States, known to gregarious Aquarians as the beginning of a new year and to the descendants of Africans exiled in America for more than 400 years as Black History Month.

For 28 days, schools around the country butcher the integral role played by slaves and their descendants in building American society. This rich history, both proud and shameful, is fractured into manageable, insulting sound bites on Harriet Tubman, Frederick Douglass and Martin Luther King. The same tracks are rewound and replayed every year.

While the American consciousness pays homage to its collective guilt, African-Americans seep deeper and deeper into the recesses of invisibility.

Somehow slavery remains an unemotional intellectual issue. Somehow the modern history of an ancient people is not afforded the dignity of being acknowledged as a systematic holocaust which continues to this very day.

Every classroom at Flynn had a display case just beside the door. When you walked through the corridors, you were exposed to a mélange of uninspired kitsch. Mrs Sasken was avante-garde.

During the month of February our display case became a triumph of free thought and poignant minimalistic expression.

We studied *Eyes on the Prize* during Black History Month. Armed with films, pictures, books and debates on the Civil Rights Movement, we undertook an excavation of America's underbelly and what we unearthed was an oppressive history so deep and so painful that we were left with no choice other than to create.

When confronted with the challenge of choosing a display for that month, of condensing our ideas and emotions into a vision that would exemplify

Room 16, we came up with one single image, that of a lone black figure casting a vote in an election booth.

On the 12th of February, the Monday following former President Mandela's release from prison after 27 years of incarceration, a newspaper clipping of a smiling free Nelson Mandela was added to our diorama.

For weeks, I passed through the doorway of our classroom to be greeted by this image. For the first time in my life, the challenge and hope of my family, my heritage and my skin were affirmed daily by my slice of America.

Lawrence Shepherd was a classmate of mine at Flynn. A sensitive, creative, compassionate and intelligent individual, I would learn a few years later that Lawrence's mother had been a drug addict for much of his childhood. Lawrence, "Squeaky" as he was affectionately known, would eventually become a small time drug dealer himself, and lose a substantial part of his youth to the correctional facilities of Rhode Island. The person who the state courts would later refer to as a "menace to society", I knew as my classmate and friend.

The Flynn Science Fair could have been held on Broadway. Each year, as the science projects got more complicated, I noticed more mothers and fathers sweating anxiously during the prize giving.

I often thought that certain parents were more deserving of the awards than their offspring.

Squeaky came to school with a glass mug filled with water. In the absence of a limestone, he had placed a pencil in the liquid.

There was an explanation about the project written in blue ink on a frayed piece of paper that had been torn from a notebook. Compared to the other projects, Squeaky's lacked the muscle and body fat of a colourful elaborate display.

When I asked him what it was about, he gently picked up the experiment and held it in the winter sunlight that shone through the window of the cafeteria cum gymnasium.

There appeared, like magic, a rainbow in the water running from the tip of the immersed pencil to the surface of the liquid.

He said, "There are rainbows hidden where you wouldn't expect, someone just has to show you where to look."

I am a poet, one who chases rainbows, and I often find them in places where my blinded eyes only saw the ordinariness of things until a teacher showed me where to look.

In the summer of 1990, after graduating from E. W. Flynn Elementary School, my family saw Nelson and Winnie Mandela along with crowds of several thousand people in New York City.

Two summers later, we would travel to South Africa and be reunited with an enormous tree of extended family for the first time. No words could ever accurately describe these events or their meaning for my life.

It is through new eyes that I am now able to look back on the expanse of night sky that is my childhood, and amongst the many beautiful shades and hues of blackness, I can also see stars: like the brave and loving members of my family, like Mrs Sasken who taught me that teaching, like leadership, is about the ability to inspire, and like a fierce eleven year old with a rainbow heart.

I am reminded, once again, that I am magic.

Devona

Devona, age twelve

Your laughter was a scab
That barred your entry
Beneath my skin of survival secrets
But I remember when we giggled a wind
That carried two black girls to the heavens
And sheilded us from the naked fangs
Of ghetto fears in our mothers' hearts
If they really knew where our nighttime words and walks would lead

To tomorrow's graveyards
Strewn with the corpses of yesterday's hopes
We lived the dreams of our once teenaged mothers
Who never laid their ghosts to rest
No one knew that we were anchored
By the weight of the dead and the living
Into classrooms where the rightness of white
Scrubbed us to the bone
And our hanging pieces of flesh
Bound us to history
And to each other
And to decay

I tied a piece of hidden flesh to my dreams
Thinking you knew to do the same

The river's rites

While travelling through Griqualand in the Northern Cape, I had the privilege of witnessing a Griqua female initation ceremony. According to tradition, when an adolescent begins to menstruate, she is kept in isolation for two full weeks where she is bathed in herbs and taught what it means to be a woman. She re-emerges as a woman in an elaborate ceremony which culminates with the members of her family and the community taking her to the river. In this ancient encounter, the river tells the onlookers whether their child is a virgin or not.

How do you build your dreams
On sand and dust
The streets will steal them
And carve them into outposts
For their lust

But when a girl's waters fall
The Griquas hear water call
From their mothers' snaking tongues
From the pride of the distant ones

Daddy's girls

One day
"Father" will be a home
In the heart
Where I call
Warmth and protection to myself
"Father"
Will push words like "no" through sealed lips
And will send sugar electricity
To muscles sweating in dance
In solitude
The voices in me will celebrate
Until I sleep
Curled up like a child
In the arms of the day and the night

Perfection sucks

If I had to spend lifetimes
Learning how to clean all of my rooms
Making my days look unlived
Where would your laughter sit?

The way we love

Being African is
Being part of an unseen force
That speaks to the mind
That created the earth
It is the knowledge
That when I speak to myself
I speak to the beginnings and endings
Of the world
So when we love
We love with the power of lifetimes
Reaching towards the infinite
We love with the fear
That the darkness in our hearts
Overshadows our light
We love through mutated eyes and arms
That stretch into the soil
To remember themselves
Love is held together by fragile hopes
That forge a path on the forgiving earth
When she bears fruit
It is with the promise
That she will never let me forget
The makings of me

The poet serves struggle to the minds of the people
Like fresh fruit to their mouths
Where poetry is sustenance
We grow strong

Two-sided self portrait

(written for a collaboration piece with Tumi Molekane)

The quiet can't contain me
In this palace beneath perception
Unmentioned are the ripples cascading
From my reflection
Unmentioned are the footpaths forged, forgotten
Demanding attention
We un-mute our tongues
We the defiant ones
We depict the rattling hums
And starve the fat back of deception

A blues not yet recorded
A two-sided self portrait
Mirrors the push and pulls of memory
Leaves my spirit haunted

A blues not yet recorded
A two-sided self portrait
Paints into sound the profound victory
I overcome this gauntlet

Drip words like juice and flaunt it
This gift is proof I was born with
A host of healers and teachers
Time free-ers unshackle the borders of mindsets
Who will you be when your prime gets
Unravelled we've travelled beyond black
Past the face of this race call your soul back

Turn up its volume in your veins
And make it clap clap to

A blues not yet recorded
A two-sided self portrait
A house of hunger is fed
When its walls can finally peak with acceptance

A blues not yet recorded
A two-sided self portrait
Every birth knows the worth of its pain
Any other foundation is nonsense

In the darkness I am fashioned
By the hands of my master
She builds me up with the might of my legacy
She breaks me down with the grace of my laughter
And when we bathe
In the waters of purpose pooling towards the shore
The currents of uncertainty
Unearth a core of light in me
And I am in exile no more

The green of words

I hear the sound of my mind
In darkness peppered with oceanic rumbles
Deeper than history
Lighter than air

An awakened mind is the thief of my sleep
I yawn,
Shake off the dust of "slam poetry" expectations
And relive the green of words
Where the world is no obstacle to my desire

The bold quiet honours me as midwife to poetry
Unpretentious
Unrelenting
Unexpected
Interpretations of the sliced days
That pass through this body

The dangerous safety of lined paper beckons
I hear myself respond
Seduced by the storyteller
I am inspiration

You and I

You and I
We are the keepers of dreams
We mould them into light beams
And weave them into life's seams

You and I
Know life is not what it seems
We strip the fat from the lean
And find the facts in between
The visions we redeem
And the agony of choice
Yours is just a mind
And mine, just a voice
But when we love
We love with a heat that rises like a song in flight
On the flesh of our backs
If it's love that we lack
Then we walk with the pain that we seek
And the love exchange that we spite
As we walk through indecision fading in fright
We ride the crest of intuition on the journey of this life

And by the hands of the infinite we hear the cries of the rest
Weighed down by their intelligence submitting to this test
But you and I
Push the boundary of reason
You and I
Plot the mystery of seasons

You and I
Paint this history to free men
Nothing can be stopped like you and I

You and I
We are the keepers of dreams
We mould them into light beams
And weave them into life's seams

I like it deep sometimes

The past does not cleanse itself
It eats inside your skull and sheds itself of your skin
And from within I've baptised burdens as my selves
I've let these limbs become my heads afraid to think of touch
Made tasting love replacing identity with a crutch

But I like it deep sometimes
Without air between breaths
With kisses to soft parts and my hair in his clench
Tears down my spine
A friend loving my behind
Makes everything too real
So I stop

I rewind the frames to claim the steps on this path
Sewed my face to plastic puppets to save my ass
To hide my weakness I was stone
Child feet played drums but I was alone
Kept thinking being black and angry meant I was strong
I've been a genius and a ho
Fat light-skinned bitch with fly Afro
First world grigamba
Pseudo black mamba without voice

And the sum of my selves, an actress,
Still plays these roles with ease
But defining my life with preconditions
Turns love into a disease

My ancestors guide these transitions
On green paths to city visions of blue beyonds
My pen and paper create the song
Where I am man
I am woman
I am God at first breath
I am a child beyond these burdens
I've got nothing left but me

And I like it deep sometimes
Without air between breaths
With kisses to soft parts and my hair in his clench
Tears down my spine
A friend loving my behind
Makes everything too real
So I stop

Insignificant

My heart does not belong to me
I am a muscle that belongs to it
I am according to its will

Pizza and red wine

Pizza and red wine
His leg moves to cover mine
Dr Phil is out the window

This is what I tell myself
As he puts my fingers in his mouth
How does he know about fingers
That lips on fingers and hands is the key into me
I am loose
Lips are wet
Lips to lips
To tongue
To hands
To neck
I am naked before no registers on any wavelength

We work on the floor like animals
Releasing without love save love for the pleasure
And respect for the being that is
Giving
Receiving
Tasting
Licking
And believing the electricity that is passing
Between hands mouths skin
I open to him

There is no condom
I'm on the pill
I am special
Are you sure
I am special
Yes
I am special
I have to be otherwise I could die for this moment
I must admit once to myself that I could die

There is something different about being with this brother
We fit together as though desire and expectation
Those failed and those fulfilled
Can be communicated through skin

He is thick enough to handle the extra pounds
But small enough to pose a challenge
I like this balance

I smoked a spliff

I smoked a spliff with Jesus Christ last night
Then leaned over and stuck my eyes inside his soul
The father let me take a journey through his pain
And beside the tears of Judas, I saw my own

J said:
"Me and man built a nation in my mind
Where God and god ruled for an eternity
The universe guided me through the in betweens
To find that people needed more than just militancy
I could provide nothing more than everything
The earth gave birth to me the flesh of natural truth
And in the hope of feeling light within themselves
I bled my love for their fear as proof
By the time I died I was an ordinary man
They made me God so they wouldn't have to do the same
I lost the pulse of humanity in this religion
But sometimes I feel it though in solitudes of pain"

But he was Jesus
And I'm a sister and I've been through more shit
Because I'm black
And life is hard in Jozi when you've got tits
So JC sparked another cone
And I told him about this brother
With the rainbow colours in his dome
My life was prayer to his rhythms
Inside him inside me

Creation was a haven in his chest
He saw me as a spirit lover sister mother
Friend in arms like no other
I saw born to be the summer in his fingertips
He in my belly made the moon rise
Where my midnight sits

And as he ravaged his way through my mind
I entertained plastic hopes to find a future in our path
But it burned at both ends
It's over now and as I sift through lies
I know I can depend on no love
For none can replace my own
And when the tears stopped falling, Jesus took me home
And then he stepped into the fury of my soul

J said:
"Love is infinite gratitude for the power of the self
Seek the answers in your own voice before you look to anyone else
Nurse the child who weeps in the valley of your suffering
Cleanse her face with ebony rains and make way for what the future brings
Teach her to make love not find love
To be love not seek love
To grow love and know love
That she might give love and receive love in due time
But don't make martyrs from the flaws of mortal kinds
Before you let another burn you, think twice
Remember no one is worth your paradise"

So maybe he was right
And maybe I am all alone
Maybe we're both fucked up

We were both definitely stoned
It's just a story about what happened last night
And how two spirits got real open
When the herb was tight

Imagination is a river of powers

We need the voices of all the people
We have ever been
To vibrate in our cells
So that we may choose from this abundance
The names for our highest aspirations

At three everything is love

Charismatic
Funny
Charming
Smart
At three the fact that he loved me
Was freedom
Africa
Family
Clear white eyes
A heart open past secrets
Cloaked expressions of something resembling kindness
In the dark with monsters ripping me apart

I was reinvented everyday
Into the girl who put out first to be played with
Who wouldn't let anyone else but him
Into her midnight conversations
Special smiles
And love
Somewhere in the sticky juicy bits
There is a love like sun-warmed honey
Standing at the spout
Daring to ooze onto thirty-year-old fingers

No one told me that I would hide
The secrets in my womb
Until love would cause me to rip off my own limbs
And send them to him as proof

That women like me do bleed
And we do love hard
Like archaic secrets that protect themselves by exposing you

I denied the three year old in me
Until I realised that I was living my entire life
As that three year old
And men would love her
As grown men children love
Selfishly

I love seeing girl children who are full of fire
I love to watch them as they walk the earth on sure feet
So sure of love that they dare anyone to defy their truth
When I see three year old girl children
I pray that they don't lose their fire

When I was three
I gave away the home inside myself
To one who was as lost as I
A thunderball of black fingers,
Grave dust
Raised up voice accelerating through politics
And Mandela
And armed struggle and lies
And Soweto in 1980 when man-love burned on women's cheeks
Just to warm in the arms of those they worshipped in the dark
In the dark I was known
In the dark I was light
And I would love in the dark for twenty years
Until I knew in the fire of my three-year-old belly
That I deserve better

If at no point

If at no point
Did you hear chantings
From places deeper
Than the caves you tread
Without my permission
Listen to the song that grows like a stalactite
On the far side of your memory
It will tell you that my heart is a mouth
Screaming razor blade sheets
Screaming eyes that never saw me
Screaming the degradation of one word invisible
NO

Tell your story

After they've fed off of your memories
Erased dreams from your eyes
Broken the seams of sanity
And glued what's left together with lies,
After the choices and voices have left you alone
And silence grows solid
Adhering like flesh to your bones

They've always known your spirit's home
Lay in your gentle sway
To light and substance
But jaded mirrors and false prophets have a way
Of removing you from yourself
You who lives with seven names
You who walks with seven faces
None can eliminate your pain

Tell your story
Let it nourish you,
Sustain you
And claim you
Tell your story
Let it feed you,
Heal you
And release you
Tell your story
Let it twist and remix your shattered heart
Tell your story
Until your past stops tearing your present apart

Taxi queen

We assume our thrones
With haphazard grace
Attached to transitions
From disgrace to any place
Regal until the destination arrives
Riding by the side of a man
Old enough to be my father
Loving me like a child
A shameful secret
Puffy and exposed
Bulging in his back pocket

On the road
I adorn him like a new shirt
While his wife's heart
Drapes the bottles he kisses
To forget her face
His children
Other lovers

I am the embryonic promise
Of a future killed by the past
A taxi queen
Riding the distance of distilled delusion
Lighting a worn road in the mind
Where he drives sorrows
Older than promises he could never ever keep
In this rear view mirror

I am a new day rising
His hand on my thighs
His eyes inside mine
Looking into a home that I could be
When I feel like home to him
I feel like I could be home to myself

I knew a girl once

I knew a girl once who lived in a house made of skin
With the spine of time stretched through it
The slightest wind would make it spin
It trapped a symphony of voices
An escalating cacophony of whirlwinds
Each one a pinpoint in time
An etched groove in her mind
But she refused to unravel
Terrified of what she might find

Instead she spent her days living from the outside in
She wore badges of silence
And learned to bend with most winds
And when the horns would blow
She'd let their fury reign from within
Protected by falsehoods and pride
A thick societal skin
But to the world she glowed
Like the moon and sun's origins
Wrapped up in someone else's skin
That's when the whispers begin
That she was coloured by incest
Coloured by date rape
Coloured by pretense
False representations
False mandates

Open your eyes
Realise when your true voice calls
That no lies will hold it within
Every day of your life a new truth you will write
But with your eyes closed you will spin

Open your eyes
Realise when your true voice calls
That no lies will hold it within
Every day of your life a new truth you will write
But with your eyes closed you will spin

Open your eyes
Realise when your true voice calls
That no lies will hold it within
Every day of your life a new truth you will write
But with your eyes closed you will spin

Sisters

I see the wisdom of eternities
In ample thighs
Belying their presence as adornments
To the temples of my sisters
Old souls breathe
In the comfort of chocolate thickness
That suffocates Africa's angels
Who dance to the rhythm
Of the universe's womb
Though they cannot feel
Its origins in their veins

Blessed am I to be loved
In the temple of my own skin
My nappy center kisses the sun
In harmony divine
Devoid of the ugly
That does not know this as God

But the sons of oppression
Never gave sisters loaves
To feed the hungry fury in their bellies
Nor did they teach them to fish for spirit

So I pray to the voices
That whisper in my soft curves
For the lionesses of my blood
To hear the songs of the cool reeds

To feel the green blood beat of cataclysm in their breasts
And to know the embrace of freedom in nourishing silences
Where their radiant ebony vessels are reflections of their souls

Ancient ones

The ancient ones plait their stories into the futures of their children
The ancient ones they use their hands to heal the backs of broken men
And I hold a pen for every ancient
Who dared not hold a fist
Against the tyranny
That sucked the life and hope out of their breasts

In ancient hands you'll find the sweat
That fuels the light in every home
The tears that bless the heartache in every story and every poem
I hold a pen for every ancient
Who built her home not out of bricks
And beat her fury into building blocks,
Made the mortar out of licks

God made hands that hold the silences
Keeping false grace in place
For a people burned to scorn
The spiritual legacy of their race
And God made hands that turned themselves into wings
Remained unseen
And used the demons from invisible realms
To wipe their sorrows clean

In every stillness, there's an ancient story
Of muti, tokoloshes and myths
And spirits who'll climb into your dreams
Creating fear out of bliss

But I hold a pen for every witch and bitch
With black magic in her genes
Who seeks to love beyond these silences
And claim back the sanctity of her dreams

Because if I as the past will be the pain of my children
If I as the present will be the shame of my children
If I as the future will call their lives a sin
I speak of things that words can kill you for
Like ancient hands calling healing back through the door

I turn my weary wounded eyes
Inward just to find
Ancient hands moulding my story from the inside
And the hands that build houses
Are the hands that beat spouses
The hands that mould my demons
Can be the very hands that free them
The hands that carry children
Build the half-truths that can kill them
And the hands that fight for freedom
Are the hands that fill this woman

And I'm not asking that you see these hands
As reflections of myself
But that you love the wells of vision
Where their deepest dreams dwell

Because there's a pen for every sister
And every mother in every home
There's a healer in these hands
That writes the lines of every poem

For every ancient who prayed
For another heavenly power to save them
There's a meditation of peace for you
In the lines written by this pen

Barbed wire

Time is a barbed wire fence
Crawling over the walls of history
Wrinkled footpaths on my granny's face
I taste the grace that laced her pace
That made them call us a forgiving race
The border between my lips and distorted disgrace
Is my morality bending
My spine refusing to break

Barbed wire sprawling through experiences
Freedom will smooth the serrated edges
Prison is any place
Where I do not see myself

Release

The mouth piece mutates
To make its evil just
In the machinery of hopelessness
The hapless place their trust
The lust of victory is slippery
Leaves trails upon the skin
Everyone is tainted by desires
Hope that your poison wins

The lies we tell can weave a spell
That holds the key to your peace
In the fabric of this madness
find the path to your release
Shape the anchors into wings
Watch every picture that you speak
In the fabric of this madness
Find the path to your release

In the land of lies
Destruction is an alibi
For those who struggle to deny
The darkness they cannot disguise
So we reach for highs in chemical creations of the light
In the rebel beats played from the sky
That call us to pay homage to the night

When all the mirrors are broken
Your parts laid out in the street
In the heartbeat that holds you together
Is the substance of your release
When sleep is the army that fights you
As you scribe your design on dreams
Dawn is the promise that guides you
Find the path to your release

Peel back my eyelids
Peel back my skin
I swim in the salts that my fathers walked before me
I wash in the balms that my mothers made up for me
When they spoke of war they spoke of what I carried in me
It is lore that I was born to change the angle of my destiny

What is l'atitude

Give me a new set of eyes
To help me see
The new state of mind that freedom brings to be
L'atitude refines the space between
The person that I am
And who I wish to be

If I was born to be a traveller with curiosity
Then show my people pushing passion pride
And let my journey be across
The spaces that divide us
The spaces that confine us
The spaces that define love
Call out and make us rise up
The spaces that create us
The spaces we must break up

L'atitude is the space between you and me
L'atitude is the space between he and she
L'atitude is the space between I and we

Wild women warriors

In October 2004 I made my first trip back to the United States after nine years to attend the Yari Yari Pamberi Conference sponsored by the Organization for African Women Writers. I had the special chance to listen to many of the voices that have inspired me along my journey.

"When the clouds clear we shall know the colour of the sky"
— *Keorapetse Kgositsile*

Wild women warriors
Work words into whirling worlds
Where writing is a rite of reason
Wisdom falls from their winds
Into my wings
In this place called New York City
That transforms human beings
Into the best and the worst of themselves
I know the colour of the sky

My kind

The land is my flesh
Forced entry forged a footpath
For my forgotten forbearers broken
And the earth severed its promise to my feet
She calls me with a voice I can hear
Past time's indiscretions
It is the fuel of her desire
That gives me heat

She whispers
"In the land of broken mirrors
There are two types of eyes
Ones that can see beyond flesh
Ones that are blinded by lies
In the land of broken mirrors
The ugly become divine
With a heart too big for this lesson
I choose to stick to what's mine
With a heart too proud for this vessel
I choose to stick to my kind"

My kind measures time
Against the steps we have taken away from God
My kind consumes each other for pleasure
My kind doesn't eat from their sweat in their prime
My kind lives closest to heaven

Beneath concrete
The earth still breathes
And she will stand
Longer than this flesh that we see
The house of man
Is painted by the tears of history
To love at all
Is our greatest endeavour